Princess Margaret
b. 1930 – 2002

Earl of Snowdon
b. 1930 – 2017
(divorced 1978)

David,
Viscount Linley
b. 1961

Serena
Stanhope
b. 1970

Lady Sarah
Armstrong-Jones
b. 1964

Daniel
Chatto
b. 1957

Charles
Armstrong-Jones
b. 1999

Margarita
Armstrong-Jones
b. 2002

Samuel
Chatto
b. 1996

Arthur
Chatto
b. 1999

Andrew,
Duke of York
b. 1960

Sarah Ferguson
b. 1959
(divorced 1996)

Edward,
Earl of Wessex
b. 1964

Sophie
Rhys-Jones
b. 1965

Edoardo
Mapelli
Mozzi
b. 1983

Beatrice,
Princess of
York
b. 1988

Eugenie,
Princess of
York
b. 1990

Jack
Brooksbank
b. 1986

Lady
Louise
Windsor
b. 2003

James,
Viscount
Severn
b. 2007

Sienna
Mapelli Mozzi
b. 2021

August
Brooksbank
b. 2021

LADYBIRD BOOKS

UK | USA | Canada | Ireland | Australia
India | New Zealand | South Africa

Ladybird Books is part of the Penguin Random House group of companies whose addresses
can be found at global.penguinrandomhouse.com.

www.penguin.co.uk   www.puffin.co.uk   www.ladybird.co.uk

Penguin
Random House
UK

First published 2023

001

Copyright © Ladybird Books Ltd, 2023
Written by Fiona Munro

Printed in Italy

The authorized representative in the EEA is Penguin Random House Ireland,
Morrison Chambers, 32 Nassau Street, Dublin D02 YH68

A CIP catalogue record for this book is available from the British Library

ISBN: 978–0–241–64320–4

All correspondence to:
Ladybird Books
Penguin Random House Children's
One Embassy Gardens, 8 Viaduct Gardens
London SW11 7BW

MIX
Paper from
responsible sources
FSC® C018179

Picture credits

The publisher would like to thank the following for their kind permission to reproduce their photographs:
Jacket (front l) Shutterstock / Daily Mail; Jacket (front r) Shutterstock / Tim Rooke; Jacket (back) Getty Images / Samir
Hussein / WireImage: 5 Shutterstock; 6 Getty Images / Intercontinentale, AFP; 7 Shutterstock / Keystone Pictures
USA; 8t Shutterstock / AP; 8b Shutterstock / Keystone Press Agency / ZUMA Press Wire; 9 Shutterstock/ Everett; 10t
Shutterstock / AP; 10b Shutterstock / David Johnson / ANL; 11 Alamy / Keystone Pictures USA; 12t Shutterstock /
Bill Cross / Daily Mail; 12b Alamy / PA Images; 13 Alamy / Keystone Press; 14 Shutterstock; 15 Shutterstock / Haydn
Jones; 16t Shutterstock / Monty Fresco / Daily Mail; 16b Shutterstock / Ted Balckbrow / Daily Mail; 17 Shutterstock /
David Bagnall; 18 Shutterstock / Mauro Carraro; 19 Shutterstock / Mike Forster / Daily Mail; 20t Shutterstock / Sipa;
20b Shutterstock / Tony Kyriacou; 21 Shutterstock; 22 Shutterstock; 23t Shutterstock / Tim Rooke; 23b Shutterstock /
Chris Jackson / WPA Pool; 24t Shutterstock / Peter Kneffel / EPA; 24b Shutterstock / David Fisher; 25 Shutterstock /
Tim Rooke; 26t Shutterstock / Jacob King / WPA; 26b Shutterstock / Alex Lentati / Evening Standard;
27 Shutterstock / Alex Lentati / Evening Standard;
28t Shutterstock / Olivier Douliery / EPA; 28b Shutterstock / Peter Morrison / AP; 29 Shutterstock / David Hartley;
30 Shutterstock / Tim Rooke; 31t Alamy / PA Images; 31b Shutterstock / T Mughal / EPA; 32t Shutterstock / AP; 32b
Shutterstock / AP; 33 Shutterstock / David Hartley; 34 Shutterstock / Jane Barlow / AP; 35t Shutterstock / Yui Mok /
WPA Pool; 35b Shutterstock / Kate Green / WPA Pool; 36t Shutterstock / Olivier Hoslet / EPA-EFE; 36b Shutterstock /
R. Nagy; 37 Shutterstock / Tim Rooke
(Abbreviations key: b-below/bottom; l-left; r-right; t-top)

HM KING
CHARLES III

A CELEBRATION

A Royal Baby is Born

Charles was born in London at 9:14 p.m. on 14 November 1948.
The first child of his mother, Princess Elizabeth, and her husband, Prince Philip, he was given the full name Charles Philip Arthur George. At that time, fathers were not usually present when a baby was born, and Prince Philip was feeling so anxious that a friend whisked him away for a distracting game of squash.

Prince Charles with his parents

Charles was born at Buckingham Palace rather than in a hospital. It was more common for babies to be born at home in those days and, as Charles's birth was not straightforward, a room at the palace was turned into an operating theatre. Amazingly, although it would have been unusual for Prince Philip to attend the birth of his child, it was expected that the Home Secretary or even the Prime Minister would be there! Princess Elizabeth's father ended this ancient custom in time for the birth.

Prince Charles of Edinburgh, second in line to the throne, was christened by the Archbishop of Canterbury. The ceremony, held in the Music Room at Buckingham Palace, took place on 15 December, when Charles was just four weeks old. Although it was a little over a decade since televisions had begun appearing in people's homes, scenes from before and after the ceremony were recorded, and crowds gathered outside the palace to feel part of such an important royal event.

Prince Charles is christened

Early Life

When Prince Charles was born, his grandfather King George VI was on the throne. The King's death when Charles was just three meant his mother was crowned Queen. This made Charles, as her eldest son, the heir apparent (the next person in line to rule). Under a charter (a rule)

King George VI with his grandson, Prince Charles

created by King Edward III in 1337, the young Charles also became the Duke of Cornwall. In Scotland, he could use several different titles: Duke of Rothesay, Earl of Carrick, Baron Renfrew, Lord of the Isles, and Prince and Great Steward of Scotland.

The coronation of Queen Elizabeth II

On the day his mother was crowned, almost a year after his grandfather's death, Prince Charles was four. The coronation took place in Westminster Abbey, where these ceremonies have been traditionally held since 1066. The young prince was under the spotlight as the three-hour event was watched by around 27 million people on television in the UK, and many millions more worldwide.

Prince Charles was educated at home by a governess (a private teacher). His parents were dedicated to their royal duties, meaning they were often away for a long time. When Charles was just five, they returned home from a six-month overseas trip and greeted him and his three-year-old sister, Anne, with formal handshakes.

Prince Charles and Princess Anne with their parents

School Years

Prince Charles at Cheam School

Traditionally, royal children did not go to school, but when Charles was around the age of eight, his parents felt that he would enjoy being with other children in a classroom. He was the first heir to the throne educated at a school.

After just under a year at Hill House School in West London, Charles was moved out into the countryside to Cheam School in Hampshire – his father's old prep school. He was a boarder, which meant that he slept at school most of the time. While there, at the age of nine, the Queen named him the Prince of Wales.

Prince Charles at prep school with friends, 1957

Charles was a thoughtful, quiet boy who found boarding difficult and was teased because his ears stuck out. He also suffered a few medical problems, having his tonsils removed in hospital and catching both flu and measles all before he was thirteen.

When it was time to pick a senior school for Charles, it was again his father's old school that was chosen. He arrived at Gordonstoun, an isolated school in Scotland, when he was thirteen. A welcome break from the school, and its cold showers and strict rules, came when he was seventeen and enjoyed two terms in Australia as an exchange student at Timbertop – a remote campus linked to a school in Melbourne, with an emphasis on outdoor pursuits. With some distance from his life as heir to the throne, Charles has said that this period was 'by far the best part' of his education.

Prince Charles at Gordonstoun

UNIVERSITY

After finishing school,
Charles was accepted
into Trinity College,
Cambridge University,
to study for a degree in
archaeology (the study
of human history) and
anthropology (the study of
people and their different
cultures). He was the first
heir to the throne to ever graduate from university.

Prince Charles visiting Aberystwyth

During his time at Cambridge, Charles cycled around
town like any other student and was mostly able to
enjoy life without too much intrusion. He played the
cello, acted in many shows with his college theatre
group and even took flying lessons!

Cycling around Cambridge

Around the middle of
his time at university,
Charles changed to
a different course
and began working
towards a degree
in history. Some
of his areas of
study were created

specially for him, and as part of this, he spent a term at Aberystwyth University in Wales, studying Welsh culture, history and language. He has often spoken about his affection for Wales and his happy memories from that time exploring the countryside and getting to know the Welsh people.

At the end of his time at Aberystwyth, on 1 July 1969, Prince Charles was formally invested as (made) Prince of Wales by the Queen at Caernarfon Castle. Charles gave a speech in Welsh watched by 4,000 invited guests and hundreds of millions of television viewers.

Upon returning to Cambridge, Charles was awarded a 2:2 degree in 1970.

Prince Charles studies at Trinity College

CAREER IN THE ARMED FORCES

In March 1971, Prince Charles flew himself to the Royal Air Force base at Cranwell to begin training as a jet pilot. As part of the course, he had to brave his first parachute jump from a plane. Almost 50 years later, Charles remembered how this jump had not gone strictly according to plan and had initially seen him upside down and tangled in the parachute's strings!

Prince Charles at RAF Cranwell

Prince Charles on HMS Bronington in 1976

Charles completed his training the following September and began a career in the Royal Navy, as had his father, grandfather and both his great-grandfathers previously. He undertook a six-week course at the Royal Naval College in Dartmouth before beginning his service on HMS *Norfolk*, a guided-missile destroyer. Charles continued to learn new skills, qualifying as a helicopter pilot in 1974. His final position in the Navy, in 1976, was two years spent as the commander of the coastal minehunter HMS *Bronington*.

Charles holds many honorary positions in the Armed Services. This means he was given the positions as an honour, without having to perform the usual duties. When he was appointed Colonel-in-Chief of the Parachute Regiment in 1977, he asked to take part in a tough training course. He explained that he could not wear the famous red beret and para wings without having completed it. Charles felt that, even though his position in the renowned regiment was honorary, he should at least be able to do some of the things that full members were expected to do for their country.

Marriage to Princess Diana

The Prince and Princess of Wales on their wedding day

Millions of people across the globe celebrated with Prince Charles when he married 20-year-old Lady Diana Spencer at St Paul's Cathedral on 29 July 1981. The ceremony was witnessed by 3,500 guests and a global television audience of 750 million across 74 countries. A further 600,000 people lined the streets of London to wave and cheer as the newlyweds and the Royal Family passed by in carriages. The new Princess of Wales wore a fairy-tale gown embellished with 10,000 mother-of-pearl sequins and a 25-foot train. In keeping with a tradition begun in 1923, the couple's wedding rings were made from Welsh gold.

Princess Diana's wedding dress had the longest train in royal history

After the service, a wedding reception was held at Buckingham Palace for 120 guests. Strawberries and cream were on the menu, and the celebratory meal was finished off with a slice of wedding cake that had been made over a period of 14 weeks. The traditional fruit cake was intricately decorated with Charles's coat of arms and the Spencer family crest, as well as roses and orchids.

After a honeymoon spent cruising the Mediterranean, the Prince and Princess of Wales returned home and began carrying out their royal duties. They lived partly at Prince Charles's newly purchased country estate, Highgrove, in Gloucestershire, and partly in apartments 8 and 9 at Kensington Palace in London.

Princess Diana and Prince Charles greet the crowds as they leave St Paul's Cathedral

Becoming a Father

Prince Charles became a father when Prince William was born at 9:03 p.m. on 21 June 1982. His brother, Prince Harry, was then born at 4:20 p.m. on 15 September 1984. They were both born at St Mary's Hospital in London. Prince William became the first direct heir to the British throne to be born in a hospital.

Another break from tradition came in March 1983, when Charles and Diana became the first royal couple to take their baby on an overseas tour. The trip was over a month long and covered 30,000 miles. Charles entertained the crowds by sharing funny stories about baby William.

Prince William waves to the crowds with baby brother, Prince Harry

A family skiing holiday

Charles enjoyed a close relationship with his young sons and always tried to be there for important milestones in their lives, from their first day at school to taking part in the fathers' race at William's sports day. As Charles himself had been educated within Buckingham Palace until he was eight, Prince William's first day at a Montessori nursery school in West London was quite a milestone. The young princes and their father shared a love of the outdoors and had many interests in common, such as polo and skiing.

William and Harry followed Charles into the military, William earning the rank of Flight Lieutenant in the RAF and working in Search and Rescue. Meanwhile, Harry rose to the rank of Captain during a ten-year career in the Army.

DIVORCE AND DIANA'S DEATH

In December 1992 it was announced that Charles and Diana were to separate. The couple were divorced in August 1996. The Princess of Wales continued to carry out her royal duties and was still considered a member of the Royal Family.

Princess Diana at the Taj Mahal, India

In August 1997, while on a private trip to Paris, Diana was killed in a car crash. Her car was being chased by photographers, and the accident happened as her driver entered a tunnel too fast and lost control of the car. Even though they were no longer married, it was Charles – along

A sea of flowers for Princess Diana outside Kensington Palace

with Diana's two sisters – who travelled to Paris to bring her body back to London. He then made his way straight back to Balmoral (the castle in Scotland where the Royal Family spend time in the summer) to be with their sons, fifteen-year-old William and twelve-year-old Harry.

Diana's funeral was held at Westminster Abbey in London on 6 September 1997. The Prince of Wales, William and Harry walked behind her coffin as the procession made its way to the abbey. Also walking with them were Diana's brother, Earl Spencer, and Charles's father, the Duke of Edinburgh.

Following the service, Diana's coffin was taken by road to her family home at Althorp, more than 70 miles north of London. During her final journey, well-wishers showed their love for 'the people's princess' by throwing flowers on to the car.

Prince Charles walks behind Princess Diana's coffin

Marriage to Camilla

The Prince of Wales married Camilla Parker Bowles in April 2005. The ceremony was held close to Windsor Castle and was a much more modest event than his first wedding to Diana. As both the bride and groom had been married previously, they decided not to make it a religious occasion. Charles was the first British royal to marry in a civil ceremony. Afterwards, however, the newlyweds were given a marital blessing at St George's Chapel in Windsor Castle. The role of best man was given to Charles's oldest son, William, who was by then 22. The couple spent their honeymoon quietly in a house on the Royal Family's Balmoral Estate in Scotland.

Prince Charles and Camilla with their children

Although a quieter occasion than Charles's first marriage, the couple were still joined by around 800 guests for the blessing service. The Royal Family were all in attendance, although the Queen and Prince Philip were not part of the civil ceremony. As his mother was Head of the Church of England, it was not seen as appropriate to attend the marriage of two divorcees, even if one of them was her son.

The wedding day

After the wedding, Camilla was known as HRH the Duchess of Cornwall. Since then, she has become involved with over 90 different charities. Her focus has mainly been around health and well-being, supporting literacy and the arts, and animal welfare.

A warm welcome for the Duchess of Cornwall

CHARLES'S GROWING FAMILY

Prince William was married to Catherine Middleton on 29 April 2011. After the ceremony, they were given the titles Duke and Duchess of Cambridge. Their first child was born on 22 July 2013. George Alexander Louis was Charles's first grandchild. William and

The Duke and Duchess of Cambridge

Catherine went on to have two more children, Charlotte Elizabeth Diana, born on 2 May 2015, and Louis Arthur Charles, born on 23 April 2018.

When Charles's younger son, Prince Harry, married Meghan Markle on 19 May 2018, they were given the titles Duke and Duchess of Sussex. Their children,

The Duke and Duchess of Sussex

Archie Harrison and Lilibet Diana, were born on 6 May 2019 and 4 June 2021, making Charles a grandfather for a fourth and fifth time. Camilla also has five grandchildren from her children of her first marriage. The couple are known to take an active role in all their lives.

In honour of his first grandchild, when Charles was 64, he transformed a piece of land close to Balmoral Castle into an arboretum (a garden devoted to trees) and named it Prince George's Wood.

Charles is known to be a loving and affectionate grandfather, playing with his grandchildren in the garden and reading to them. He sees less of Archie and Lilibet as Harry and Meghan have made their home in the USA.

Prince George with his father and grandfather

CHARITY WORK

As the Prince of Wales, and now as King, Charles has links with hundreds of charities. He supports both large and small organizations, helping the important work they carry out to be recognized. He and other members of the Royal Family are patrons of over 3,000 organizations. Being a patron means they give their name and time in support.

Prince Charles paying tribute to the work of Samaritans

Prince Charles celebrating the work of Marie Curie

When he was the Prince of Wales, Charles was patron of over 420 charities. He helped attract funds and publicity to the causes he supported, which in turn led to higher donations. It is thought that he helped raise around £140 million a year for good causes. He visited the charities regularly and showed a keen interest in their work.

Charles's charity work really began in 1976 when he left the Royal Navy. He used his severance pay (money given to those leaving the Army, Navy or Royal Air Force to help them in their new lives) to set up the Prince's Trust. A charity still close to Charles's heart, the Trust aims to help deprived 11–30-year-olds to improve their lives. It has helped to support almost one million young people across the UK.

Young people from the Prince's Trust with Prince Charles

Climate Activism

Charles made his first speech about the environment in 1968, aged 20, seven years before the common term 'global warming' had been created. He was ahead of many people in his thinking when he tried to draw attention to the pollution of our seas, rivers and even the air we breathe. For decades he used his high profile to encourage us all to think more about conservation (the protection of nature) and the dangers of climate change (human activity causing worldwide temperatures to rise).

Prince Charles's environmental work in action

Prince Charles admits to talking to his plants

As the world slowly caught up with Charles's ideas, he continued to appear at conferences to make speeches, always trying to give more attention to the importance of protecting the world around us. Charles has recalled that he was thought of as a 'complete idiot' when he made his own farm organic in 1986. An organic farm is one where animals and crops are cared for without the use of harmful chemicals. He has also fitted solar panels on Clarence House in London (his official residence, or home, when he was Prince of Wales) and at Highgrove, in Gloucestershire, to create his own electricity using the power of the sun.

Charles has often spoken of his wish to leave a better world behind and feels a sense of duty to protect our natural world for the generations to come. He explained that he did not want to be accused by his children or grandchildren of not doing enough to try and make this happen.

THE ROYALS ON TOUR

As Prince of Wales and now as King, Charles is one of the UK's most high-profile ambassadors (or representatives). He travels regularly overseas to represent the UK. Royal tours also provide an opportunity for him to better understand international problems and issues, as well as meet other Heads of State (e.g. presidents or monarchs) and senior officials. His tours within the UK help to shine a light on achievements and local issues, and try to encourage good relationships between different faiths and communities.

Prince Charles with priests at Akshardham Temple, India

Up until 2023, Charles had made official visits to Australia sixteen times, Canada eighteen times and India ten times. He had also visited 45 of the 56 Commonwealth countries. The Commonwealth is a group of countries, many historically connected to the British Empire.

Prince Charles on tour with Queen Elizabeth in 1970

Prince Charles first began taking part in Royal tours when he was barely out of his teens, visiting New Zealand and Australia in 1970. He and his sister, Anne, joined the official trip with the Queen and the Duke of Edinburgh.

Planning a Royal tour is complicated. Charles usually takes up to fourteen people to help him, including bodyguards and office staff. The tour can last just a few days, or up to around two weeks, depending on where in the world the visit is happening. Each day is planned carefully by either the UK government or the hosting nation and includes meetings, activities, special meals and events.

Prince Charles at Fatima Jinnah Univeristy, Islamabad

CHARLES'S MOTHER

When Charles's mother was crowned Queen, he was only four years old. The immediate increase in her workload, including long tours abroad, meant she was often separated from him (and his younger sister, Anne) for long periods. As the children were left in the care of nannies and governesses, it appeared that the relationship between the Queen and her oldest son was more formal than we would expect today.

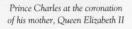

Prince Charles at the coronation of his mother, Queen Elizabeth II

The choice of school for Charles must also have contributed to some difficult years. While Gordonstoun may have suited his father, it was not a good fit for Charles's

The Queen and Prince Charles in conversation

personality. It was also a long way from home. As Charles grew older and his duties increased, he appeared to grow closer to his mother. As heir to the throne, Charles often attended engagements with his mother, learning more about the role he would one day take over. There are many photographs that show them laughing together, and it certainly seemed that their relationship deepened as the years passed.

The Queen was always keen to support Charles, and his second marriage to Camilla helped their relationship to develop further. Camilla and the Queen enjoyed spending time together and shared a love of horses and the countryside. She publicly stated that it was her 'sincere wish' for Charles's second wife to become Queen Consort when he ascended the throne.

Prince Charles and the Queen sharing a joke

THE DEATH OF THE QUEEN

Queen Elizabeth at Balmoral Castle aged 96

When the Queen died, aged 96, at Balmoral in September 2022, Charles and his sister were at her bedside. At the very moment of her passing, Charles became King and his wife, Camilla, became Queen Consort. His eldest child, Prince William, became heir to the throne and was soon after made Prince of Wales.

The new King and Queen Consort returned to London the day after his mother's death to meet the Prime Minister, and then flew back to Scotland to accompany the Queen's coffin to St Giles's Cathedral in Edinburgh. In the eleven days between the Queen's death and her state funeral, they toured the Home Nations (England, Northern Ireland, Scotland and Wales), greeting crowds of well-wishers. Alongside other members of the Royal Family, they also hosted gatherings for politicians and Heads of State. Charles took just one day over this time to grieve and reflect in private.

King Charles addressing the nation on the death of Queen Elizabeth

The Queen had been on the throne for 70 years, celebrating her Platinum Jubilee just three months before her death. She had ruled for longer than any other monarch in British history – in what has become known as the second Elizabethan era. Charles referred to her death as 'a moment of the greatest sadness for me and all members of my family'.

King Charles in military uniform at the funeral of his mother, the Queen

Charles Becomes King

When Charles became King, he was 73 and had been heir to the throne for seven decades – the longest wait in the history of the British monarchy. As Prince of Wales, he was able to give his views on subjects close to his heart, such as climate change and architecture. He had the freedom to be outspoken as he tried to make a difference. However, as monarch this is something he must avoid. The King must be seen to show no favouritism to any cause or political party.

King Charles III

Westminster Abbey, London

Although Charles became King the moment his mother died, he was not crowned until 6 May 2023. The coronation is a symbolic religious ceremony held in Westminster Abbey, where British kings and queens have been crowned for nearly 1,000 years. The new King took the 'coronation oath' during the service. He was anointed (touched) with holy oil and had the St Edward's Crown placed on his head. This crown, in use since 1661, is made from solid gold and is decorated with precious stones and gems – including rubies, amethysts, sapphires, garnet, topazes and tourmalines. It is part of the Crown Jewels and is often on public display at the Tower of London.

Being King-in-waiting for such a long time has meant Charles has gained a lot of experience and knowledge to help him in his new role. He has met many foreign leaders, many Prime Ministers and, through his charity work, he has some understanding of life for ordinary people. He is the 62nd monarch to serve over the last 1,200 years.

Prince Charles meets President Obama at the Oval Office in 2015

THE HOUSE OF WINDSOR
DURING THE REIGN OF CHARLES III

King Charles III
b. 1948

Diana Spencer
b. 1961 – 1997
(divorced 1996)

Anne,
Princess Royal
b. 1950

Mark Phillips
b. 1948
(divorced 1992)

Camilla,
Parker Bowles
b. 1947

Timothy Laurenc
b. 1955

William,
Prince of
Wales
b. 1982

Catherine
Middleton
b. 1982

Henry,
Duke of
Sussex
b. 1984

Meghan
Markle
b. 1981

Peter
Phillips
b. 1977

Autumn
Kelly
b. 1978
(divorced
2021)

Mike
Tindall
b. 1978

Zar
Phill
b. 19

George,
Prince of
Wales
b. 2013

Archie
Mountbatten-
Windsor
b. 2019

Charlotte,
Princess of
Wales
b. 2015

Lilibet
Mountbatten-
Windsor
b. 2021

Louis, Prince
of Wales
b. 2018

Savannah
Phillips
b. 2010

Mia Tindall
b. 2014

Isla
Phillips
b. 2012

Lena Tindall
b. 2018

Lucas
Tindall
b. 2021